The Space Between Us

*poems & paintings
by Elaine Ellis*

PRESS

CALGARY, CANADA

PRESS

The Space Between Us: Poems and Paintings.
Copyright © 2019 by Elaine Ellis.

All rights reserved. No part of this book may be used or reproduced, except for brief quotations in articles or reviews, without written permission from the author. For information, visit elaineellis.ca.

ISBN: 978-1-9994721-0-8

I am deeply grateful to my family and friends who provided much needed insight and encouragement during the creation of this book.

*to those who are crying now—
you will be comforted*

*to those who believe the truth
is harder than the lie—
may you be set free*

Contents

Prologue

Now—

Silent	7
Cold	8
Numb	10
Still	11
Shake You	12
Questions	13
Anger	14
Regret	15
You	16
Wondering	17
Now	19
Surreal	20
A Picture of You	22
Sirens	24
The Autopsy Report	25
Scream	26
Breathe	28
Sadness	29
Alone	30
Quiet	34

Then—

Climbing	39
Loud	40
Ember	41
Numb	42
Fighting	43
Impatient	44
Anger	45
You— The Real You	46
Motormouth	47
Memories	48
Drowning	52
Addict	53
Premonition	56
Gravity	57
Poppies	58
Laughter	60

When—

Whole	63
Grace	65
Incorruptible	67
No More	70
Hard to Imagine	71
When	72

Epilogue

Prologue

Hello?	
	Hello—
	There—
	There was a collision—
What?	
	There was a collision.
Oh.	
She's okay?	
	She's okay—
	No—
	She crossed the line—
What?	
	She crossed the—
Yeah—	
But—	
She's okay?	
	She's okay—
	No.
	They had to cut her out—
What!	
	They had to cut—
But—	
She's okay?	
	She's okay—
	No—

                          There—
                          There was no pulse.

What?

                          There—
                          was—
                          no—
                          pul—

You're kidding, right?
This must be false.

                          No—
                          Hello?
                          Hello?
                          You okay?

I'm okay—
No.

                          I'm sorry—

What?

                          I'm sorry—

Yeah.

                          I—
                          I gotta go.

What?

                          I gotta go—

Oh.

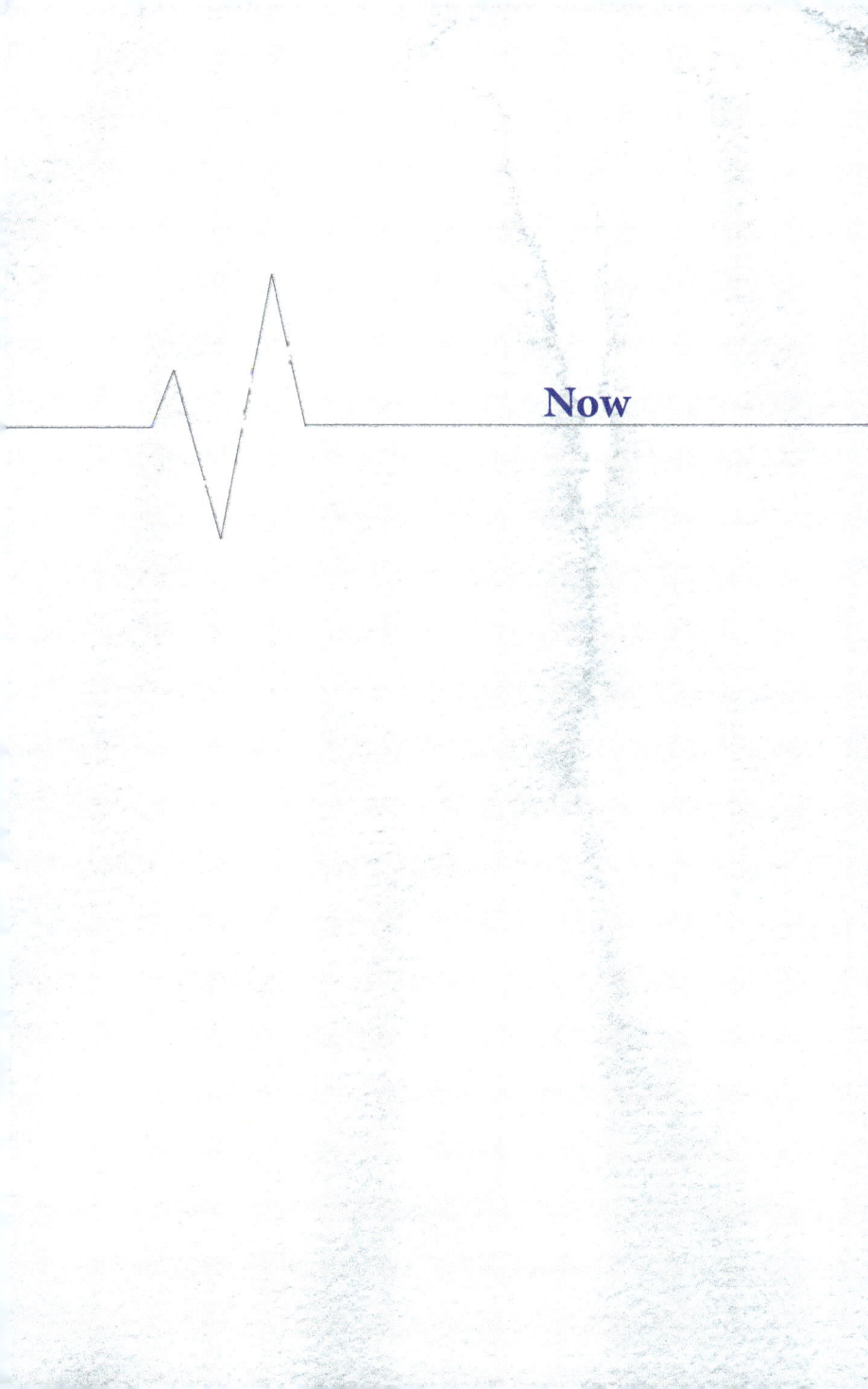

Silent—
Wasn't sure what to say

Silent—
Would it have mattered,
Anyway

Silent—
A Reign of Silence
Existed
Persisted
Between us

Silent—
What would you say

Silent—
If you knew about—
Today

Silent—
You are silent

Jesus!
Oh so silent

Nothing but
Silent—
Now

Cold—
　Fingers
　A body with no soul

Cold—
　A shell
With no host home

Cold—
　Uh
　　Poor
　　　Likeness
　Of
　　One

One—
　Who never ran
Cold

One—
　Who now lies
Cold

Cold—
　In
　　The
　　　Ground—
Cold

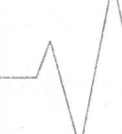

Numb—
Me

Numb—
Them

Can't feel
Won't feel

Not now
Crazy how

We're all—
Numb

Still—
You are still

Can't move
Won't move

Still—
Everything is—
Still

Things move
Around me

Around you
But we—

We are—
Still

Shake you
  I wanna
Shake you— Right now

Wake you
  I wanna
Wake you— Right now

Make you
  I tried to
Make you— See how
A— wake
  For you
  Was gonna
Be like— Right now

Make you
  I wanna
Make you—

Shake you
  No matter
How I— Shake you

Can't
  Wake you

Can't
  Ever
Wake you— Right now

Questions—
So many questions

Why—

When—

How—

Can't ask them now

Anger—
Towards you

Anger—
Towards them

Anger—
Towards Him?

What for?
Won't change

Pain remains
Your remains—

All we have
Now

Regret—
Should've

Regret—
Could've

Regret—
Would've

Borrowing time
Yesterday for today

But—
Tomorrow—

Won't change—
Now

You—
You've left a hole
A gaping hole
Right in the middle of—
Us
All our pictures
Bear its mark
Now

You—
You've left a riddle
A puzzling riddle
Right in the middle of—
Us
All our thoughts
Bear its hark:
What—do—
We—do—
Now

Back to life
Back to work
Try not to be a jerk—
Perhaps a joke
With other folks
But—
All—
Without—
You

Wondering—
Did the stars align
Or simply
Collide
That day

Wondering—
Did you fall asleep
Or simply
Misjudge
That line

Wondering—
Did you feel much pain
Or simply
Awake
On the other side

Wondering—
Did you pause to think
Of all of us
Before everything
Hushed

Wondering—
Just wondering—
Now

Flowers—
Breathtaking flowers
Arranged all around
Poised just so
Never more to grow
Beauty—
And—
Ashes—
Now

Surreal—
Not real—

Can't grasp
What's passed

We're living
Somewhere
Between
The earth
And
The sky
Now

Surreal—
Not real—

Knocked round
By a breaking bullet
That's just
Whizzed through
From
The
Great
Big
Blue

Surreal—
Not real—

Walking round
In a daze
Can't discern
The truth
In this haze
Wondering
How
You got trapped
In this maze

Surreal—
Not real—

But —
As time
Passes

Surreal—
Becomes
More real

You start to feel

And reel

As surreal
Becomes
More real
Now

I saw a picture of you
Today

She stared at me
With weathered eyes
But
Like a Bad Samaritan
I almost passed her by

Until
Her mute moves
And silent shame
Played
Upon my heart strings

Returning
With comparative compassion
I mumbled some jumbled words
Fumbled some cold cash
Tried to help her see
How to get free
In light of you and me

Grazing
Her outstretched hand
Resolve quickly turned to sand
And my skin began to crawl
At what I then saw
The stark exposure
Of her makeup-caked scars

Turning
From her broken grin
I thanked God
You were with Him
As I shuttered
At this picture of you
Today

Sirens—
Your shrill shrieking—
Impossible to ignore

Sirens—
You penetrate our very core

Sirens—
Whose demise
Do you now howl
Whose world is about
To be turned round

Sirens—
Silent prayers
Counter your incessant call
For unknown strangers
Now
Under
Your merciless maw

Lying there
A white sheet
Forever stained
With the contents of your blood
Living proof
Of why
You're not here
Like a scalpel
It severs
The jugular of our hope
As if
We didn't already know
The axiom of the matter
But we
Needed it
Signed in blood
To shut up
The dissension in our heads
Now
Examine the foreign terms
Probe the medical dross
Unfold
The heart of the matter
Can you
Even pronounce it
Oh God
No way
To ever renounce it
Now

Scream
I wanna scream
Right now

Let loose
The pantheon of unruly emotions
I'm grasping by the throat

Jammed, crammed
Packed way down
They're starting to
Claw, maw
Surge back up

They're groping for the key
That'll free
That frail creature
Shut up
In the confines of my dark,
Dank throat

Once free
She'll gulp cool, fresh air
And wail
Golf ball sized hail

But I fear
It won't end quite there

When these unruly emotions all escape

Everyone around is gonna feel the quake

Like Jesus clearing the temple
Righteous chaos is gonna rule

Triviality—
She'll be blown away
With one mere puff
Before she can utter
Any more useless stuff

And Materialism—
She'll be knocked down
Her empty towers
Will all crash to the ground

Bureaucracy—
His miles of paper piles
Will be scattered to the four winds

And Greed—
Won't even know what hit him

When these pent up emotions
Claim free reign
Embodied in
One
Big
Piercing
Scream

Breathe—
Just breathe—
Brought to our knees
Oh God—
Teach us how
To breathe—
Just breathe—
Now

Sadness—
It's etched on my face
I carry this picture
From place to place

A torrent of tears
Has carved the valleys
Over the years

If you trace the tear's course
You might find the source
But the remedy—
It's further upstream

Sadness—
It's etched on my face
I'd like some other emotions
To take its place

Some rolling hills
And crow's feet
That could speak
Of happier times
And the days of nursery rhymes

But, sadness—
It's etched on my face
Determined to take its space
Now

Alone
All alone
I walk
This darkest of valleys
Alone

Full
Of blind want
To
Fly far from here
Yet, desiring
Thy rod; Thy staff
Where comfort
Is, was, shall
Doubtless be

Alone
All alone
I walk
This longest of valleys
Alone

Lost
In this fog
Where
Nothing, no one
Wholly attends
My contrite call
For
This lonesome vale

Seems
My cross
Now
To bear

Alone
All alone
I walk
This hardest of valleys
Alone

I
Used to skip
Such
A gazelle-like step
Now,
I plod, plod
E'er I plod
For what earthly cause
I cannot truly tell

Alone
All alone
I walk
This surest of valleys
Alone

Not sure when
I'll find
That celestial stair

And, haply ascend
This dark, damp dungeon
Leave long behind
These shifting shadows

Until then—
Help me find rest
In green pastures
Kissed by your light
And, lead me
By still waters
For my soul's delight

Alone
All alone
I walk
This destined valley
Alone

Oh God
In your mercy
Take this cup
Of suffering
Far from me
But if
That cannot be
Take my hand
Lead me through
This desolate land

Let my life and my pride
Be poured out
Once again
By your side
May I find
Renewed purpose
As your bride

And may this cup
I now drink
In Your name
Lift me from the brink
May it quench
The very fires
Dancing all around
Because this valley
Is but a shadow
Ahead—
Is Jacob's hallow

Quiet—
Everyone is quiet—
Now
Not like—
When
Condolences
First
Poured in

Quiet—
Everyone is quiet—
Now
Avoiding me
Like the plague
Cause
They simply
Don't
Know
What to say

Quiet —
Everyone is quiet—
Now
Perhaps
They think
We've moved on
Cause life
Goes on
And private
Concerns

Drone
On

Quiet—
Everyone is quiet—
Now
In my darkest
Hours
I gather
Whispers
Others scatter
That the pain
Doesn't cut
Quite
As deep
Given
That we're
All
Bound
By the rule
Of the ground—
What
You sow
You're
Gonna reap

Even so
Despite
What they may
Or may not

Say
The pain
Clamours on
And
We
Certainly
Haven't
Moved
On

Then

A swing set
A big grin
A young, determined chin
Full of promise
Nothing broken
Climbing up and over
Back then

Loud—
Laugh out loud
You used to be so
Loud

Loud—
Stuck out of the crowd
Let the grief shout
Now—
Loud

Hot—
You were
Hot—
Red hot—
A live wire
A raging fire
Could burn, shock, alarm you—
Don't provoke
Or get too close
But
Hot—
Toned down
Nothing to fear
When treated dear
Can be contained
Restrained
A love to warm you
A fire that protects you
Enchants you
Can't you—
Fire—
Who put you out
A spark—
A flame—
Wish they remained

Numb—
All you wanted to feel
Was numb
Emotions—
Numb
Life—
Numb
Regret—
Numb
Just numb
Didn't you ever think—
It was—
Well—
Kind of—
Dumb
Just wanting to be—
Numb

Fighting—
We were always
Fighting—
Like cats and dogs
Back then
Not sure
Why
We were at war
Your passion
Would knock me to the floor
I'd quietly shut the door
If opposites attract—
We should have been
Magnets
Unable to separate
But we—
Drifted
Apart
Oh—
For the chance
To mend—
Or, even—
Have—
A good, old-fashioned
Fight

Impatient—
You were impatient.
Had to be first—
Never wait your turn.
First to kiss—
First to risk—
First to go through that one way door.
Hope you found what you were looking for.

Anger—
Towards me

Anger—
Towards them

Anger—
Towards Him?

What for?
Won't change

Pain remains

Gather
The remains

Cast off
Your chains

Try
Another refrain

Stop
Casting the blame

Learn
To dance in the rain

You—
You weren't the same
A stranger with your name

You—
You wouldn't have wanted
A motherless child; a childless mother

You—
You stopped coming round
Nowhere to be found; no common ground

You—
What happened to you
You were gone long ago
A shadow, a ghost

Even so
Kind of wish
That pale shadow
That frustrating copy of—
You
Still remained
Then
We could—
We would—
Try to summon
You—
The real you
Back home

Motormouth—
Remember
We called you—
Motormouth
Wasn't quite pleasing
But, we were only teasing
Cause
You filled the room
With constant chatter
Before
The serious matter
Miss that sound
No longer to be found
The continuous hum
That cheered all glum

Memories—
So many memories
Buried deep
In a sea of years

The number that include me and you
Must exceed the grains of sand
On the shore
Yet—

The same ones
Keep washing up
On the banks of my recollection

Amusing anecdotes
Bitter betrayals
The same simple
Fragments
Litter the beach
Like common broken shells

But—
I'm searching
Among the sands of time
For the giant conch shell

Beautiful—
Unfractured—
I want to press my ear against
The smooth iridescent

Cavity

And hear it whisper
All the secrets that lie hidden
In an ocean of years

Listen to the gentle refrain
That will clearly explain
The gravity
That binds my heart to yours

Despite the years—
Regardless of the tears—
In spite of the form
Or substance
That makes the moon as unlike the ocean
The magical conch
Will gradually reveal
The force
That pulls my heart to yours

In spite of—

The

Space

Between

Us

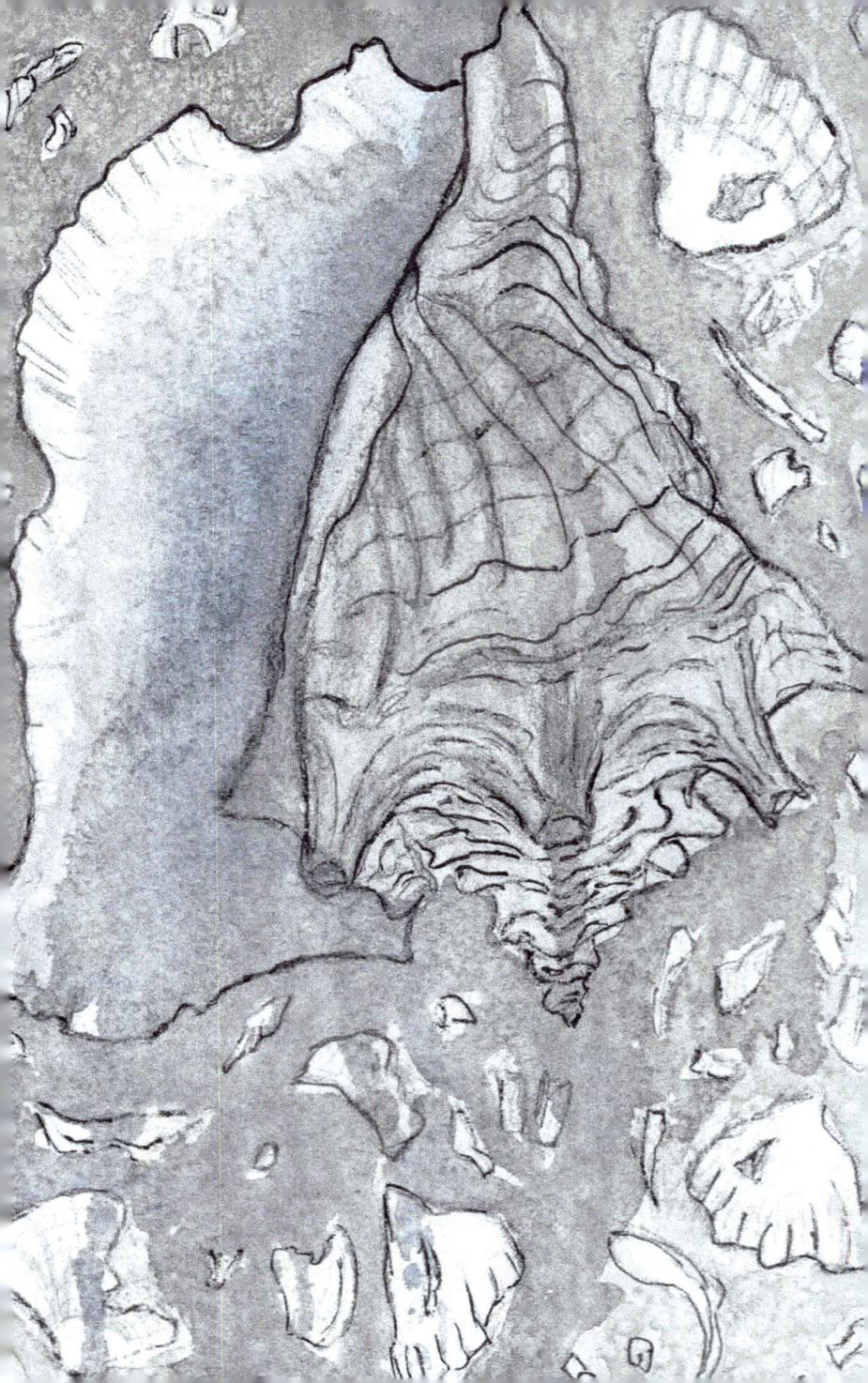

Drowning—
Did you know you were
Drowning—
Back then—
A sea of lies
Another guise
In too deep
Falling asleep—
Tried to wake you—
Wanted to make you
Recognize your state—
Never quite sure about your mate
But none of us knew how—
Doesn't much matter now

Addict—
Gotta
Get your fix
Usin'
A lot of—
Little tricks
Changing
Like a chameleon
When symptoms
Are on the rise
I'm searching
For the truth
Among
The litany of lies
Not possible
To see it
In the glaze
Of your eyes

Junkie—
Runnin'
All around town
Nowhere
To be found
Looking
To escape
From
An opioid rape
Forcing
You

In a contorted cage
Where
You can only swing
From counterfeit calm
To roaring rage
Never dreamed
You'd be a junkie
But
Just can't
Get rid of
That clawing monkey

Addict—
Who
Let you down
Grounded
All your hope
Thinking
You gotta be
High
Just
To get by
Can't
You look around
See
Your coping
Isn't sound
Stop
Demanding
We let you be

Admit
You lack the key

Don't
You wanna be free

Open
Wide the door

Let
Your dreams
Once
Again
Soar

Premonition
I had a definite
Premonition
Back Then
Despite that foreboding feeling
I did
Nothing
Lying here
Staring at the ceiling
Wondering
Why
You
Forgot
How to fly
Wondering
How
I
Could've
Helped
You
Now
But
All my tormented tears
Can't replace
The wasted years
Back then

Gravity—
　Like gravity
　　You were destined
　　　To fall
　　　　When
　　That corrosive compound
　　　　First entered your cell walls
　　　　　Not sure when or how or why
　　　　It became
　　　　　　The Apple
　　　　Of your eye
　　All that's certain
　　　Is that within
　　　　　That forbidden fruit
　Lay a pernicious worm
　　　That consumed all of you
　　　　Leaving behind an insatiable ghost
　We were unfit to rightly restrain
Plunging head first into a deadly domain
　　　You were no longer familiar
　　　　　With even your own name
　Cause it rewrote your life's verse
　　Forever changed its natural course
　Derailed all your dreams
　Cancelled all your potential
Cause no one knew how
　　To reverse or even reconcile
　　　　Gravity's
　　　Downward
　　Spiral

Poppies—
Your favourite flower
Known for their seeded power,
And that famous verse
Where poppies blow
Between crosses, row on row
How fitting—
Poppies marking graves—
Not only for the braves,
But others—
Beyond Flanders fields and verse
Who are sleeping now,
Poppies—
Were their curse.

Laughter—
Remember—
Before it was December—
You filled the room—
With infectious
Laughter.
Can't quite hear it—
Hard to feel it—
Want to be near it—
Laughter.

When

When
 We
  Lowered
   You
    Down
     Into the cold, bleak ground
      Everyone wished
      That you would rest in peace
       As if
       All we can hope
        For
        Is some kind of
         Bliss
         Full
          Slumber
             But I imagine
            You've landed
         On your feet
     You're dancing
       Somewhere
          Way up high
             Just over the sky
 You've traded all your earthly scars
     And life's dimly lit bars
           For a kingdom
    Of newly made priests
         And it isn't dour
          In God's bower
         You're enjoying
            A most majestic

                    Feast
            Drunk on the wine of Heaven
And a Spirit that gives
                More than it takes
    A life that leaves you
            Perfectly full
            You happily surrender
                A will
                        Now
                    Made
                        Whole

Grace—
Thank God—
For
Grace
When we finish this race
And stand face to face
At that pearl of a door—
We'll all want in—
But—
On account
Of our sin—
Not one—
Not even one—
Will get in—
Except—
The Holy One—
Who lends us
Grace
Oh God—
Thank God—
For
Grace

You've entered
That celestial door
Found
Much more
Than
You
Ever
Bargained for

Seeing
Your Maker
Face to face
Wondering
How you ended
In this place

Overcome
By majesty
Of such
Colossal size
Trembling
In enlightened
Inadequacy
Tongue-tied
With downcast
Eyes
You fall
To your knees
Ready to plead
But this Lion of Judah

This Lamb of God
This Guardian of Heaven
Amazes you more
When such fierce beauty
Chooses to stoop
And lift
A pauper
Now
Keenly aware
Of her peasant state
Out of the mire
Place you
Away from the fire

He chooses
To establish you
Among the stars
Welcomes you to reside
On victory's side
To dwell
Among angels
And saints
And furthermore
Abstains from
Reproach
Scorns shame
Consumes chains
With one gentle,
Fiery look
This King of Kings

This Lord of Lords
Then
Invites you
To a most majestic feast
Treats you
Like a long lost
Daughter
Crowns
You
With His righteousness
Declares
Your sins are no more
Bestows on you
A kingdom
Simply
Incorruptible

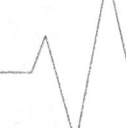

Tears—
No more
Fears—
At the door
Joy—
Forevermore

Hard to imagine
You—
Now—
Living—
When
All we have
Is
Then—
But
Someday
I'll know—
Someday
I'll see—
You and me—
When—

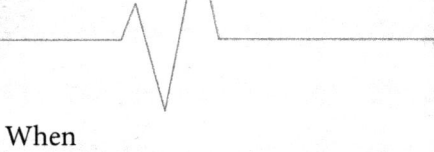

When
Now = Then
It will
Be
When

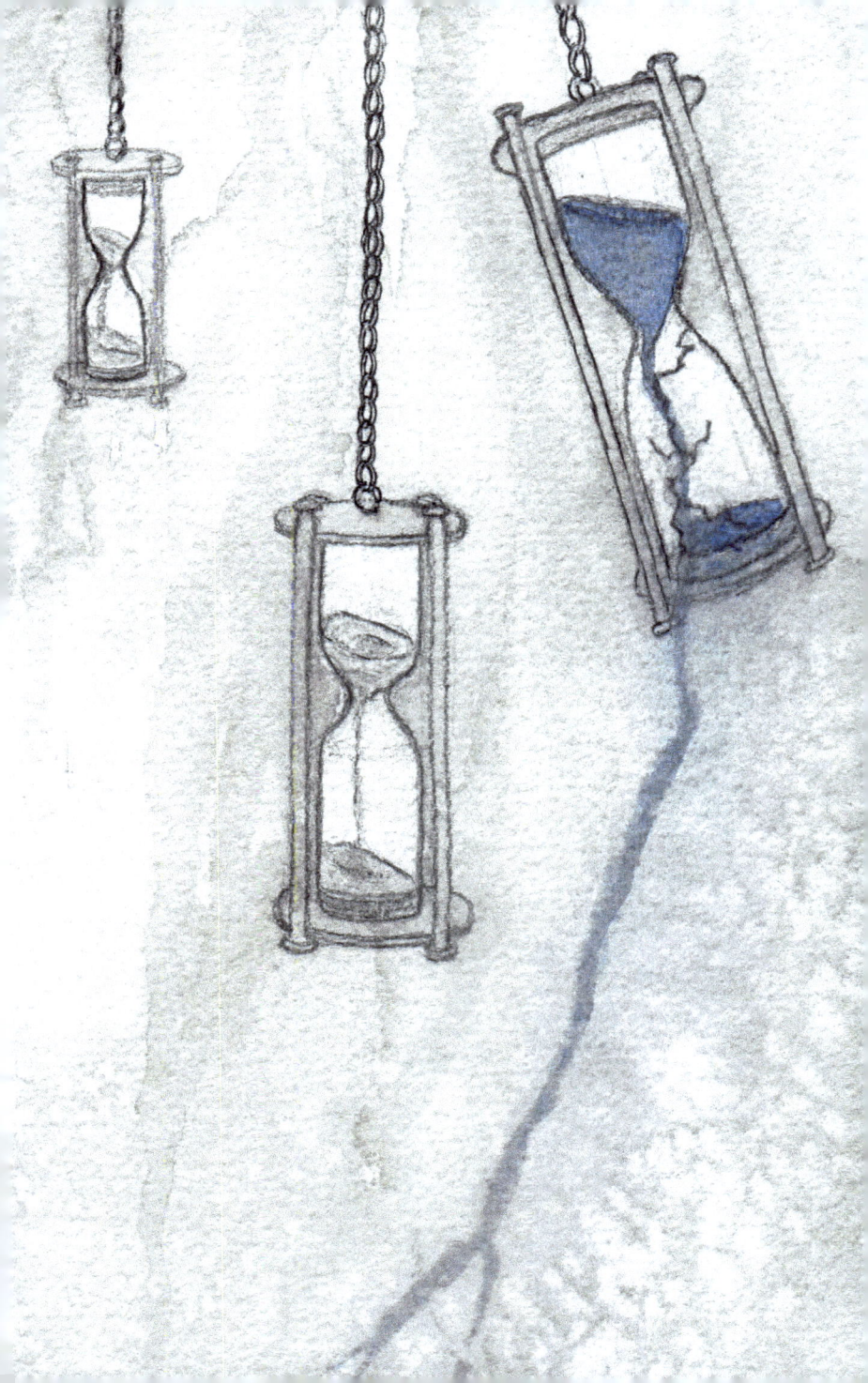

Epilogue

Victim
Who is the victim
In this

A lively girl
Dearly loved
Though dearly loved
Perhaps
Once
A little too nearly
Loved

Victim
Who is the victim
In this

A headstrong teen
Dearly loved
Though dearly loved
Perhaps
Once
A little too freely
Loved

Victim
Who is the victim
In this

The self-same teen
Dearly loved

Though dearly loved
Almost dies
Hears
Baby's cry, feels perhaps
A little too fiercely
Loved

Victim
Who is the victim
In this

A wide-eyed bride
Dearly loved
Though dearly loved
Perhaps
Once
A little too merely
Loved

Victim
Who is the victim
In this

A sick woman
Seeks help
From money hungry
White coats
Prescribed
Pills, perhaps too easily
Loved

Victim
Who is the victim
In this

A broken soul
Dearly loved
Though dearly loved
Casts blame
Creates
Chains increases pain, hides
Love

Victim
Who is the victim
In this

A fractured family
Dearly loved
Though dearly loved
Shuns shame
Starts
To vacillate blurring
Love

Victim
Who is the victim
In this

A bound woman
Dearly loved

Though dearly loved
Steals, lies
Feels
Anger toward suspicious
Love

Victim
Who is the victim
In this

A drug dealer
Someone loves
Though solely loved
Sells soul
Increases
Death toll, much too blindly
Loved

Victim
Who is the victim
In this

A rash woman
Dearly loved
Though dearly loved
Crosses line
Feels
All alone in dying
Love

Victim
Who is the victim
In this

A young driver
On her side
Though not at fault
Crushes car
Feels shock
In newly entangled
Love

Victim
Who is the victim
In this

A heavy boy
Dearly loved
Though dearly loved
Looses early
Mother's elemental
Love

Victim— Who is the victim
Culprit— Who is the culprit
Victim— We're all the victim
Culprit— We're all the culprit

In this

With over two million Americans dependent on or abusing prescription pain pills or street drugs, the United States is undeniably in the throes of a national opioid epidemic.[1] The death toll due to overdoses continues to rise.[2] Provisional numbers from the Centers of Disease Control and Prevention show that over 49,000 people died in the United States in 2017 due to an opioid related overdose.[3] That is an average of 134 deaths each day—a number that exceeds 2016's record high and is a 4.1-fold increase from 2002.[4] To put that into perspective, the number of deaths due to opioids now exceeds the number of deaths due to car accidents[5] or breast cancer.[6]

Canada is also facing a national opioid crisis.[7] The increasing number of overdoses and deaths caused by opioids, including fentanyl, has been declared by the Government of Canada to be a public health emergency.[8]

Opioids are powerful drugs formulated to reduce chronic or severe pain by replicating the pain reducing properties of opium, derived or synthesized from opium poppy plants.[9] They include the legal pain killers prescribed by doctors, like codeine, oxycodone (Percocet), hydrocodone (Vicodin), morphine, and fentanyl, as well as illegal variations like heroin and illicitly produced fentanyl.[10]

The long-term effectiveness of opioids for managing chronic pain contrasted to the risk for dependence, tolerance, and addiction is questionable.[11] Many people become dependent on opioids and experience withdrawal symptoms when they stop taking the pills.[12] Tolerance usually accompanies dependence, meaning that opioid users have to take larger and larger doses to achieve the same effect.[13] People who develop a dependence on pain pills may switch to street drugs like heroin because it is less expensive[14] or because they can no longer obtain a valid medical prescription.[15] In fact, according to the National Institute on Drug Abuse, 80% of heroin users first misused prescription pain pills.[16]

With such troubling statistics, we need to be keenly aware of the risk factors related to opioid misuse. According to the Mayo Clinic, America's top-rated hospital, "Anyone who takes opioids is at risk of developing addiction."[17] They do not view opioids as safe and effective for long-term pain management and advise that opioids are safest when used for three or fewer days to manage acute pain, like pain following a bone fracture or surgery.[18] Patients who need to take opioids for acute pain are advised to take the smallest dose possible and for the shortest time needed and to only take the medication as prescribed.[19]

The Governments of Canada and the United States are responding to the opioid crisis with new legislation, programming, and research,[20] but a concerted effort from the citizens of both countries is needed to end this crisis. The public needs to be properly informed of the risks associated with using opioid medications and people and families struggling with opioid use disorder need to know where to go for help and that it is necessary to talk about their struggles— no one can fight this alone. People with opioid use disorder need medical help to wean themselves off of opioids as the withdrawal symptoms can be severe.[21] They also need help understanding underlying issues that lead to addiction. Mostly, in order to fight this crisis, we have to fight first against the stigma and shame often connected with addiction. As the Government of Canada states, "This is a complex health and social issue that needs a response that is comprehensive, collaborative, compassionate and evidence-based."[22]

Endnotes

1. "Opioid Crisis Fast Facts," *CNN* online, last updated June 16, 2018, https://www.cnn.com/2017/09/18/health/opioid-crisis-fast-facts/index.html
2. "Overdose Death Rates," National Institute on Drug Abuse, revised August 2018, https://www.drugabuse.gov/related-topics/trends-statistics/overdose-death-rates
3. See "Overdose Death Rates," note 2.
4. Ibid, note 2.
5. Gillian Mohney, "Deaths from Opioid Overdoses Now Higher Than Car Accident Fatalities," Healthline, published March 30, 2018, https://www.healthline.com/health-news/deaths-from-opioid-overdoses-higher-than-car-accident-fatalities#1
6. Nadia Kounang, "Opioids Now Kill More People Than Breast Cancer," *CNN Health* online, posted December 21, 2017, https://www.cnn.com/2017/12/21/health/drug-overdoses-2016-final-numbers/index.html
7. "Responding to Canada's Opioid Crisis," Government of Canada, accessed October 3, 2018, https://www.canada.ca/en/health-canada/services/substance-abuse/prescription-drug-abuse/opioids/responding-canada-opioid-crisis.html
8. See "Responding to Canada's Opioid Crisis," note 7.
9. See "Opioid Crisis Fast Facts," note 1.
10. Ibid, note 1.
11. Mayo Clinic Staff, "How Opioid Addiction Occurs," Mayo Clinic, accessed October 3, 2018, https://www.mayoclinic.org/diseases-conditions/prescription-drug-abuse/in-depth/how-opioid-addiction-occurs/art-20360372
12. See "Opioid Crisis Fast Facts," note 1.
13. Ibid, note 1.
14. Ibid, note 1.
15. See Mayo Clinic Staff, note 11.
16. "Understanding the Epidemic," National Institute on Drug Abuse, accessed October 3, 2018, https://www.cdc.gov/drugoverdose/epidemic/index.html
17. See Mayo Clinic Staff, note 11.
18. Ibid, note 11.
19. Ibid, note 11.
20. See "Opioid Crisis Fast Facts" and "Responding to Canada's Opioid Crisis," notes 1 and 7.
21. See Mayo Clinic Staff, note 11.
22. See "Responding to Canada's Opioid Crisis," note 7.

www.ingramcontent.com/pod-product-compliance
Lightning Source LLC
Chambersburg PA
CBHW061730070526
44583CB00024B/3080